Prayer

The Source of
Strength for Life

Grace Dola Balogun

This book is a power source
for living through prayer.
You will learn how to put all
of yourself in the hands
of the living God.

Prayer

The Source of
Strength for Life

Grace Dola Balogun

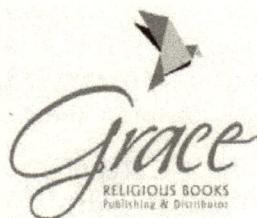

Grace
RELIGIOUS BOOKS
Publishing & Distribution

Grace Religious Books
New York, NY

Prayer

Scripture quotations are from the King James Version of the Holy Bible.

Grace Religious Books Publishing & Distributors books may be ordered through booksellers or by contacting the publisher:

Grace Religious Books Publishing & Distributors, Inc.
213 Bennett Avenue New York, NY
10040
www.Gracereligiousbookspublishers.com

To contact the author: 1-646-559-2533
info@gracereligiousbookspublishers.com

ISBN: 978-0-9851460-1-6 (epub)
ISBN: 978-0-9851460-2-3 (pdf)
ISBN: 978-0-9851460-0-9 (sc)

Library of Congress Control Number: 2012933417

Printed in the United States of America

*I dedicate this book to our Lord
and Savior Jesus Christ, the One
and only incarnate Son of the Father,
full of grace and truth. He is the
mediator of a new covenant who
listens to and answers prayer.
To Him be the glory, honor, power,
praise, majesty, dominion, and
adoration now and forever.
Amen.*

Contents

Preface

Our Lord said in Matthew 21:21-22, "I tell you the truth, if you have faith and do not doubt, not only can you do what was done to the fig tree, but also you can say to this mountain, Go throw yourself into the sea, and it will be done, If you believe, you will receive whatever you ask for in prayer."

When we are going through trial and tribulations, in any difficult times, disappointment of any source, and during hardships, we must pray that God the Father Almighty who sent His only Begotten Son into the world will bring good things to pass with His love for us through His Son Jesus Christ.

We must also exercise strong faith and courage to desire the best from the Lord. When we are desperate with our situation, we must turn immediately to the Word of God for answers and comfort in tribulations. Find courage to pray until the heavens open and God answers that prayer.

The Holy Bible teaches us through so many stories of God's purposes how He fulfills His Will, how He triumphs over all the work of evil, such as hatred, violence, wickedness, etc. and how God brings great changes and blessings to His people by the power of the Gospel of Christ. The Bible also enlightens our hearts, reminding us how God fulfills His promises in the lives of His people when God's people pray in confidence to Him.

God also works supernaturally when we pray according to what God has spoken about in the Scriptures. We must allow God to restore the desires of our hearts and fulfill them if He knows that our heart's desires are good for us.

My prayer is that this book will bring great changes into the lives of those who read it, no matter what church denomination, and also in the heart and mind of other people of different religions and religious perspectives and beliefs all over the world.

Prayer

1

Lord, Teach Us How to Pray

In Luke Gospel Chapter 11: 1-13 and in the
book of Matthew 6:5-14, during the time of
Our Lord's earthly ministry, He was praying in a certain place. When He finished, His prayer
was so inspired that one of His disciples said to Him,
"Lord teach us to pray, just as John taught His disciples." Jesus said to them, "When you pray, say:
"Our Father who are in heaven,
hallowed be your name, your
kingdom come your will be
done, on earth as it is written in
heaven. Give us today our daily
bread. Forgive us our debts as
we forgive our debtors. Lead us
not into temptation and deliver
us from evil. For thine is the
kingdom, the power, and the
forever."

Our Lord indicates the area of concern that all the body of Christ must concentrate on in a Chris- tian's prayer. Our Lord said believer's greatest concern in prayers and in our lives should be the hallowing of the name of God. It is the utmost important that God be reverenced, glorified and exalted in our lives.

In our prayer and in our daily walk we must be intensely concerned with the reputation of God, awareness of who God is in our lives, in church, His gospel and His kingdom.

We must pray for the kingdom of God on earth now and with its ultimate fulfillment in the future. We must pray for His Will to be done in our lives which means that we must sincerely desire God's will and purpose to be fulfilled in our lives and the lives of our families, relatives, and friends according to His eternal plan.

Believers must determine the will of God pri- marily in His revealed infinite word, the Bible, and through the Holy Spirit's leading in our hearts and mind.

We should pray for our daily bread and needs. Our prayers must be concerned sins and willingness to be able to forgive those of who trespasses, or have done any form of evil against us. Believers must pray for deliverance from the enemies, Satan's enmity and evil its evil purpose, we must pray for deliverance from his power and schemes and all his tricky games in believers mind and soul.

Our Lord Jesus Christ emphasizes that all Christians must be determine, ready, and willingly to forgive the evils from the other Christians and the unbelievers around us. God is saying to us if we do not forgive those who offended and willfully do wrong to us,

He will not forgive us our offenses, and our prayer will not be able to ascend to Him. All the believer of God must take this warning of our Lord seriously to heart by forgiven those who hurt them. We have more than six or eight forms of prayer request to the Lord.

Three of these prayers are concerned with our holiness and the will of God for us. The other three pertain to and concerns with our personal needs.

Our Father in heaven means that our prayer connects us with our heavenly father. As our father, the Almighty God loves us, cares for us, and He always welcomes our fellowship and intimacy.

Through Christ our Lord we have access to God our father at any time either to worship Him and communicate all our needs to Him. God is a father of holiness who opposes sin and all unrighteousness.

He does not tolerate evil. As our heavenly father, He disciplines and blesses us; He will withhold as well as give us what we need. Even things we do not know that we need. God justice and mercy is incomparable. He responds to all His children according to our faith in him as well as our obedience to him. The most important concern in our prayers and in our lives should the hollowing of the name of God.

In our walk with God and our prayer to Him we must be focused and concerned with the reputation of God, His church, Gospel and His kingdom. Our prayer must be based and concerned with the kingdom of God on earth now and with its ultimate fulfillment in the years to come.

Our prayer must be based on Christ return on earth and the establishment of God's eternal kingdom in the new heaven and the new earth. We must pray for the Holy Spirit's presence and manifestation of the kingdom of God now and forever.

Our Lord Jesus Christ demonstrates God's power and authority over Satan and demons and plundered his possessions with the power of prayer and His communion with God the father when he was conducting His ministry on earth. It is impossible to remain neutral in the spiritual realm and conflict between Christ's kingdom and the power of evil.

Many people who decided not to follow Christ, set themselves up against Jesus Christ and His righteousness, or they are on the side of Satan and the ungodly.

Jesus' words indict any attempted spirited neutrality or compromise with unrighteousness and disobedience. All the believers, body of Christ and all the household of faith must be delivered from sin; they must renounce sin totally in their lives.

They must be committed to the life of obedience, prayer, and righteousness. They must be filled with the Word of God every day by so doing they be will filled with the power of the indwelling of the Holy Spirit. Believers must know that after their conversion, Satan's power does not end but continues, it never-ceasing.

We are safe from sin and Satan if we are fully committed to Jesus Christ using all the necessary means of Grace th a is available through the word of Christ. Where sin abound grace abounded more and more by His grace we are saved.

Believers of Jesus who have been delivered from all demonic and were clean by renouncing all sin in their lives if they should leave the door open for more evil spirits with the increase of evil influence to come to them will fall back into serious sin.

It's like someone that was wash clean, and put on white robe, later decided to go into the coal mine, for the white robe to be completely clean as before will be very difficult, or impossible. I urge all the believers to learn how to be ready to pray at home, and in our churches.

Prayer

2

What We Need in Prayer

What we need in prayer is confidence to approach the throne of grace. When we pray, we are calling upon the name of the Lord Jesus Christ; we are placing our dependence and trust in God the father, God the Son, and God the Holy Spirit.

We are pouring out our heart and soul to him, and letting Him know that he is the only one our Deliverer in the time of affliction, distress, and all forms of disappointments, and in time of troubles and tribulations.

We need to pray to seek His strength and His power over all our trouble soul. We must call upon God in prayer and reminded him that we are a sinner, undeserving of mercy, but he saved us and bless us with His mercy and love. We must remind him about His great love for us, and His goodness and mercy that followed us through all our lives, His unceasing protection in the past and throughout our lives.

7

As children of God, we must ask that he listen to our prayers and answer our prayers according to His will and infinite mercy. When we pray, we are strengthening are trust in the Lord and we are exercising our unshakable faith in Him.

We are also obeying His commandment because God commanded us to pray therefore, we pray in response to God's loving invitation. Our Lord said, "Ask you shall be given." Through prayer our worries will be reduced or erased to the point that it will not border us anymore. The most essential care for worry is our prayer.

Through prayer we renew our trust in the Lord Jesus Christ's faithfulness, we cast all our problems upon him, who cares for us God's peace comes to keep and guided and lead our hearts, mind and soul, spirit as we commune with our Lord. God wills continue to strengthen us in order to do all the things for us according to His will. Prayer helps us to connect and receive the peace of God that surpasses all understanding. (Phil. 4:6-7).

Believers must rejoice in the Lord Jesus and gain strength by recalling His grace and promises. The Bible said that we restyled against spiritual warfare with the help of the Holy Spirit's power. We are Christian soldiers, we must fight against all the power of evil, not in our own power but with the power of the indwelling of the Holy Spirit (Eph. 6:18).

Prayer shows our dependence upon God's power and His infinite wisdom, what we need in prayer is powerful tools so important that we will be completely surrender to the Lordship of Jesus Christ and let Him know that we cannot do anything for ourselves, and we have no strength or power to solve this problem on our own. He is the only one who can help us.

What we need in prayer is to show that we are complete in Christ, and we are acting as we supposed to act as a child of God. We must ask the father for everything, even up to drinking water, we must pray that the water go down safely in our throat to our stomach.

All believers need to communicate with the father and tell him what is in our minds. Even though God has the power to read our mind, He still wants us to come to h im as His child and humble ourselves and let Him know what we are going through, what we needed, even though he understand our situations far-ther more than we are thinking or asking, He wants us to maintain an intimate relationship with Him as His child His children with complete trust.

What we need in prayer is a heart full of praises to God the father through our Lord Jesus Christ who give us His Spirit, the Spirit of holiness, and the Spirit of prayer. The more we praise Him and acknowledge what He has done in our life, what he is doing right this moment in our lives and what He will continue to do in our lives, the more the heart of God rejoices with us, and the more he is ready to do more and more great things in our lives.

We praise the Almighty God when we acknowledge His greatness, mercy and love in our lives, His provisions, His power of healing all our diseases, His power of protection from all evil from day one we arrived on this earth. His innumerable company of angels that he sends to us every day to protect us while we sleep or in danger.

Believers need to praise him for His mercy, goodness and love that follow us everywhere we go every day of our lives. The Bible said if it is not the mercy of God we would have been consumed His mercy failed not it's been renewed every morning great is thy faithfullness Lord our God.

What we need in prayer are praises and adoration, proclamations of His holy names in our prayers. Praises him for who he is and for what he continues to be in our lives by calling His holy names in your prayers.

A mighty fortress is our God, the Almighty God, Compassionate, gracious Loving God full of truth and righteousness, Lord God Almighty Father, Son, and Holy Spirit ever one God; The very God the true God, the Creator of everything that exist in heaven and on earth, the only Blessed ruler of human souls, the one who have immortality in the light, the immortal, the invisible the only wise God.

The Lord Jesus Christ full grace and truth, the Lords of Lords and the Kings of kings, the Holy one of Israel, the Seed of David, The bright and the morning star. The ascended God, the God of resurrection eternal live, the one and only who ascended into heaven, and sited at the right hand of God the father Almighty, the Lamb of God who took away the sin of the whole world, the incarnate begotten Son of the Father, the Holy child of Bethlehem, Our crucified Lord, our risen Lord, the great shepherd of the sheep, the good shepherd, the Chief Shepherd, the one and only our Hope of Glory who is coming back to judge the quick and the dead and all the eye shall see Him.

The one and only the way the truth and the life, the giver of life. The Messiah who came to this world and redeemed us from our past, present and future sins, our gracious master and our great redeemer, the light of this world the true light that shines forever, and no darkness can comprehended it.

The mediator of a new covenant, our prophet, priest and High priest of a new covenant, the mediator of a new covenant, the mediator between God and Man. Our advocate of a new Covenant, the one and only Jesus Christ our Lord same yesterday today, and forever. When we call on His names, our heart rejoice and shows how glorious great is our God, God of love, God infinite mercy, God of great infinite compassion, compassionate gracious loving God.

The book of psalms full of prayer of praises to the Lord who is the great I am. If we believers pray the prayer of praise we will be full of happiness and rejoice, our heart, mind and soul will magnified the Lord.

Our heart will rejoice in God our Savior who has done and continues to do great things in our lives Holy is His name forever. Our heart will be full of peace of God that surpasses all understanding and we will be stronger in the Lord and in His almighty power.

What we need in prayer is the heart and mind of thankfulness at all times. God will be able to do more great things in our lives. The fruits of our lips are given thankfulness to His holy name.

We need to thank God before we sleeps and thank him when we wake up in the morning because He is the one that make us to sleep and wake up.

We must give thanks to God for the food we eat, for the good health that he gave us, we must thanks God for our physical health, and spiritual standard because in him we move, and we have our being.

He clothes us with His goodness, righteousness and love. The holy Bible said for God so love the world that he gave His one and only begotten Son that those who believed in him will not perish but have everlasting life. (John 3:16). He provides for our clothing and shelter, he also surrounded us with good people in our lives that help us when we were down and in distress they take care of us.

We must continue to give God thanks every day of our lives, he bless us with His peace that pass all understanding he save us from perils of danger, disasters, accidents, violent behavior from some people around us. He fills our heart and mind with joy everlasting. We must continue to give him unceasing thanks.

What we need in our prayers is to confess our sin if we know we violate His orders or commandments telling him we are sorry for what we do or have done. Especially when we intentionally hurt someone feelings physically or emotionally know that no matter what they are, God created them in His own image.

By telling God about our sins, we put our trust in him that he will restore us back into the fold as our Lord's parable of prodigal son. (Luke 15:11-21), verses 17-19, "When he came to his senses, he said, How many of my father's hired men have food to spare and here I am starving to death I will set out and go back to my father and say to him, Father, I have sinned against heaven and against your I am no longer worthy to be called your son; make me like one of your hired men." Our Lord said God and the angels rejoicing in heaven with great love, compassion and grief for those who have fallen into sin and spiritual death but when one sinner repents they rejoice.

The book of Isaiah 62:5 said, "As a young man marries a maiden, so will your sons marry you; as a bridegroom rejoices over his bride, so will your God rejoice over you." God is never silent. He has appointed watchmen on the walls of Zion, prophets and faithful intercessors who never stop praying for the establishment of God's kingdom on earth and for the Glory of Jerusalem.

We, the body of Christ, need to be diligently pray without ceasing for the establishment and the return of our Lord Jesus Christ on earth in order to set up His kingdom that Christ will rule with righteousness over all the earth.

What we need in our prayer is the power of prayer for the great commission to be fulfill through the help of the holy spirit through all the believer of Jesus Christ for all the believers to work hard for the great commission sincerely, so that all the elect of God will be save and Christ will return without delay.

We must also pray for our neighbor, our friends, those who are in government. We need to pray for the judges who are making tough decisions in the lives of individual who do wrong.

We must pray for our enemy so that God can turn them from our enemy to our friends. We must pray for those who are violent among us, for the Lord to turn them into peace, for the peace of God to rule

14

and continue to rule in their heart and mind always so that they can live a peaceful life.

We must pray for those who hate us for our Lord to turn them from hatred in to love, for them to see the light of God penetrate into and through their hearts and fill them up with joy of the living heart.

God told prophet Jeremiah 32:41, "I will rejoice in doing them good and will assuredly plant them in this land with all my heart and soul." God surely gather all the children of Israel from all the Lands God told prophet Jeremiah that the people would be restored to the land and to a right relationship with Him, and he will make an everlasting covenant with them. God did exactly what He said in 1948, is anything too hard for the Lord? The answer is No.

Of the Father Almighty, father of our Lord and Savior, the father of all glory, sustainer of all things assured prophet Jeremiah that through His power the people would be restored to their land. Up until today God's power of love never stop, or diminished for His people from individual people, to the people in the community, for the nations and for the entire universe. God's Word promises a blessed future for all believers in Christ Jesus our Lord.

Believers in Christ must and can depend on God's Word even though we may not know the specific manner, or how His promises going to be achieve or takes place, or how it will be accomplished. But we must

Continue to trust, and have strong faith in the Lord. We must believe that the good work He started on our lives, He is the only one that can carry it out to the completion according to the power that works in us. God hears the prayer of the righteous.

Because of our sinful nature, we are powerless to make ourselves righteous and acceptable to come before God in prayer, we have to know that Jesus Christ is the only one that lived this earth sinless, His death and resurrection, declares us righteous, Jesus carried all our sin on the cross.

His righteousness is ours by faith with this in mind, we are confident and boldly approach the throne of grace, where God hears and answers all our prayers.

The holy Bible says: "There is only one mediator between God and man, the man Christ Jesus our great intercessor in heaven. Christ is the only one who died on the cross for our past, present, future sins and rose from the dead, who is now sited at the right hand of God, who defeated death and the power of evil and sins.

The same Jesus Christ is the only one that sited at the right hand of God interceding for us. Asking the Father for what we needed and the time we need it. Jesus Christ is our high priest of a new covenant in heaven, He knows and familiar with all our suffering, weaknesses, temptations, afflictions and troubles. When we call on God the father in prayer through our Lord Jesus Christ's intercessory holy name we must know that we have the assurance and the confidence, and boldly we will obtain mercy and find grace to help in time of all our needs (Hebrews 4:16).

We must all approach the throne of grace with confidence because Jesus Christ our suffering Lord sympathizes with our weaknesses, we can confidently approach the heavenly throne, knowing that our prayers and petitions are received and desired by our heavenly father. It is the throne of grace because from it flows God's love, help, mercy, forgiveness, wisdom, spiritual power, spiritual gifts, the fruit of the spirit, the river of living water, and all that we need in any circumstances of our lives.

We need to abide in Christ. Jesus Christ explained to us that the key to a strong and healthy Christian life is abided in him. (John 15:1-7). Jesus stated that I am the true vine, He describes Himself as the "true Vine" we are the branches, by remaining attached or clued to him as the source of our live, and power, we produced fruits. God almighty the father is the Gardner who takes care of the branches in order that they may bear fruit and more fruits into His kingdom. Our Lord Jesus Christ speaks of two different branches: the branch that is fruitless and the new branch that is fruitful.

The branches that stopped to bear fruit are those that no longer have life in them that comes from enduring faith in and love for Christ. These branches the father pulled from the vine, He separates them from vital union with Christ.

When people or a believer stopped remaining in Christ, they cease to have life in him thus they are severed and thrown into the fire. The branches that bear fruit are those who have life in Christ and in themselves because of their enduring faith in and love for Christ these branches the father prunes so that they will become more and more fruitful.

3

Pray Through
the Word of God

In order to be strengthened in our prayer lives we must pray through the Word of God. When we quote the Word of God in the Bible what he said to back up our request our supplications, our heart desires in our prayers to Him, we are praying through the Word of God.

When Christ's words abide in us, the spirit of our Lord Jesus Christ takes control of our thinking our decision makings, our prayer lives our relationships with friends and our children, families, relatives and as well as in our neighborhood.

Christ's word is always alive and living in the hearts minds, and soul of believers. Christ word changes our values and it's also re-arranged and reestablishes our life priorities. For example Jesus Christ our Lord stated in His words,

"Ask it shall be given you, seek you shall find, knock the door shall be opened, to whom asked received and to whom knock the door was opened to them." (Luke 11:9-10). With this word in our mind, it shows us that our Lord encourages prayer without ceasing with perseverance in our prayers.

We must continue to ask, and keep on asking, seeking and knocking. When we continue asking it implies our consciousness of our need and our strong belief that God hears our prayer. Seeking also implies earnestness in our petitioning with our obedience, while we continue to exercise our patient and obedience to Christ's will for our lives.

In our continued knocking it also implies that our perseverance in our dependence on the Lord, even if He does not answer our prayer at the time of our need. Because in the mind of God, His answer is either wait, this particular request is not good for you, or I have something better than what you are requesting in your prayer.

We have to know that God is the all-knowing, all powerful, omnipotent, which means God have the power to do all that we think is impossible. There is no limit to His power and perfection of the true power of God.

Omniscience, means that our God have the ability and power to know everything infinitely including our thoughts, our feelings everything about lives and the entire world. He is the all-knowing all-powerful, He knows everything on earth and under the earth, and omniscient means God have the power and ability and quality of being every-where.

A divine power of being present everywhere at the same time, He can appear in all places at the same time. All merciful and mighty God. We have to know and remember that Christ's blessed assurance to us who ask will receive what they ask is based on our responds to seeking His kingdom, recognizing that God is our father in heaven who is full of goodness mercy and love.

Who never change and will never change. Our answer to prayer is also based on God's will for our lives, how we worship and fellowship with Christ and importantly, our obedience to Christ's commandment.

Jesus Christ stated that our father in heaven will not fail His children who diligently seek Him day and night with all their hearts. He loves us more than any earthly father (vs. 11).

He wants us to come to Him in prayer to ask him for whatever we need, he promise to give us what is good for us and he desires to provides solutions to all our problems and provide for our food with the help of the holy spirit who is our helper *paraclete* heavenly quest comforter, and counselor.

Believers must learn to pray for life's necessary provisions according to our Lord's will, call on the

Lord and act in our life according to His fatherly love for us, we must also ask for things that will help us to enhance the kingdom of God on this earth.

When we pray through the Word of God, we pray about the things that will give him glory and exulted is holy name, things that will help us in our walk and in Christian service, as well as church ministry.

We have to realize that when we abide in Christ and His Word, it is automatic what we request in prayer according to His Will will be done. (1 John 3: 18-21) apostle John in his writing stated: "Dear Children, "let us not love with words or tongue but with actions and in truth. This then is how we know that we belong to the truth, and how we set our hearts at rest in His presence, whenever our hearts condemn us.

"For God is greater than our hearts, and he knows everything (vs. 21) Dear Friends, if our hearts do not condemn us, we have confidence before God (vs. 22) and receive from him anything we ask, because we obey His commands and do what pleases him."

John was telling us in his writing that the reason why some prayers were answered and some prayers were not is because we of devotion and our relationship with the Lord effective prayer is based on our obedience, love, as well as doing what is pleasing in God's sight at all times. Our Lord Jesus answers prayers based on His word and His work of redemption in us.

When we approach God in prayer with His words, we should not let our prayers be based on who we are, or our position as pastors or elders, millionaire, poor, adult senior citizens, or children. Our prayer to God must not base on what we think or what we have achieved for Christ through our ministry.

We must humbly, boldly and confidently call upon God through prayers by first confess that we are unworthy, and pray with a humble heart, we come for God's mercy which is been renew every morning with His faithfulness and goodness.

We must come to God with the heart of exultation of His holy name, proclamation of the gospel of God our prayers may not be answered if we pray to God with wrong intension and motives, asking for what we needed without asking for the needs of others around us.

We express our love when we sincerely help other people who are in need by sharing our earthly good with them. When we refused to give other people who are in need of food, clothing, shelter, or money and medical help who in need, we close our hearts to them we pretend that someone else should help them, or using our money to enhance the work of the ministry so that other people might be save and the gospel of God be preach to those who are in darkness by not having the gospel preach to them.

The Word of God consists of God revealing something about himself through His spoken word, which is ultimately and perfectly personified in His Son our Lord Jesus Christ. The Word of God is the means by which He created all things (Genesis 1:1). "In the beginning God created the heavens and the earth." By this word, God spoke and heaven and earth were created. This confirmed and firmly established God's supremacy over the whole of creation.

He created all things by His spoken word, God reveals himself to us through His word, and His word is an important instrument of divine power and revelation. Therefore, when we quote His word in our prayers we are acknowledging that His word is powerful and we trust in His word and power. As well as showing that God's Word will be fulfilled in our lives according to His divine plan and according to His Word.

Jesus Christ is the Word of God and God's saving plan for creation. The Word of God makes the creation known and the Word is God. Jesus Christ is equal to the Father as the supreme authority over all creations; the gospel of Jesus Christ is the fulfillment of the Word of God.

Therefore, Jesus Christ is coming back into this earth; He is our hope of glory according to the Word of God. God's Word is creative, perfect, with supreme authority, and is the Word of life.

When we quote His Word in our prayers we connect the power of God with our prayer, and our prayer ascended straight to His throne. The Word of God come to Moses at Mount Sinai Ten Commandment and Law also the Word of God is natural, sustained, redeemed, and consummated. God said " My word that goes out from my mouth will not return to me void, but it will accomplish what I desire and achieve the purpose of which I sent it" (Isaiah 55:11).

God's Word is creative, powerful, perfect, and is all-sufficient, especially our Lord Jesus Christ is the incarnate begotten Son of God. We must pray with the Word of God in the scripture. To remind him of what He said in the Old Testament, and in the New Testament and in the life to come world without end.

4

The Word of God
Cleanses Us

Believers need the Word of God cleansing from all unrighteousness. Our Lord said, "you have been clean through the word that I have spoken to you" (John 13:3-8).

As Christians, we walk through this world, we contact many things that can cause defilement onto us, such as listening to unholy talk, looking at unholy pictures or advertisements, working with ungodly people that does not care for things of God, living among ungodly people whereby, if they hear you praying they can be playing loud music in their house, or apartments or playing any form of immorality song. The cleansing takes place by the water of the Word of God.

As we read and study our Bible every day, or hear preaching and teaching of the Word of God, and as we discuss the Word of God with one another in the church or in our home with our church friends; the Word of God cleanses us.

We find that the Word of God cleanses us from all the evil influences and temptation that might come upon us. If we neglect and stop reading the Bible not staying in the Word of God, we are giving room to the evil influence to remain in our minds and building up a room for temptation.

We must stay in the Word of God which lives and abide in us cleans us from any evil and any immoralities, cleans us from any things that can contaminate us. Our fellowship with our heavenly father and the Lord Jesus Christ can be maintained by the continual efforts of the cleansing action of the word of the scriptures in this life. The cleansing we received at the time of salvation is the cleansing from our sins through Jesus Christ our Lord is once in a lifetime.

While cleansing from the pollution of sin takes, place continually through the Word of God. Reading and studying the Word of God help us to stay close to the Lord and abide in His will and it will help us to exercise forgiveness, strong faith as well as strengthens our prayer life.

God's Word is the living word that we must use in our daily prayer as the traveler's map, the pilot's compass, the pilgrim's, the solder's sword and the believer's rock of salvation. The Word of God is light to our path to direct us, comfort, console us; the Word of God is spiritual food to sustain us.

The Word of God cleanses us full of wisdom to teach us, fire to warm us from cold disappointment of the world. The Word of God opens the heavens, restored the paradise, the Word of God teaches us that there is hell and hell fire, which burn thousand years.

The Word of God reveals the mind of God to man and show us the way of Salvation, the Word of God is true and holy cleansing the spirit soul and body from any unrighteousness, God's glory is reveal the love of Jesus Christ is the Word became flesh and dwell among us, we behold His glory, the glory of the only begotten Son of the Father full of Grace and Truth.

Praying in the Word of God will bring great light to our prayers. Praying with the Word of God will add more power to our prayer life; it will bring us closer to the Lord in prayer. It will open the door that the enemy will not be able to close, because when God's Word opens the door, no one is more powerful than God; therefore, the Word of God will make great things Happen in our life, that none and no power of the enemy can open it.

Praying in the Word of God will allow God to perform His miracle in our lives. Miracle of healing, any diseases, miracle of financial blessings in so many ways that we cannot think, or imagine. Blessings of great wisdom, knowledge and understanding in an immeasurable abundantly, exceeding way. Praying with the Word of God will helps us to think beyond our present state or situations.

Praying in the Word of God will fills our heart with the light of the Holy Spirit penetrating through our spirit soul and body, energizing our spiritual power strengthens our faith, trust, and love in our Lord Jesus Christ.

Praying in the Word of God will help us to create mind of forgiveness we will be able to forgive those who trespasses against us. We will be able to pray for our enemy as well and we will see the result that our enemy turns around to be our friend.

We must pray with the word of Christ and be specific in our asking, seeking and knocking request in our prayers. We must allow the word of the scripture to guide our hearts in our specific prayers to the Lord.

We must pray to God, to help us to triumph over any work of evil, any work of darkness, any work of danger that threatens the lives of His children.

We must pray with our mind, focus on the things that bring great joy to our life. Pray for people who are in the hospital on diverse diseases, illnesses that there is no cure, or any form of cure for God's intervention in the lives of such people.

This is the specific prayer. We must pray for job seekers so that they can get a job in a miraculous way with God's power and mercy enabling them, directing them to a specific area where there is job opening and they may be hired.

For the Lord to bring healing to the lives of the sick among us that He will reveal His great glory and ever ending love to them. After their healing so that they can be useful for God's glory, bringing the message o f salvation to those who does not know him. (Isaiah

35:1-6), "Be strong, do not fear, your God will come." "Then w i l l the eyes of the blind be opened, and the ears of the deaf unstopped. Then will he came leap like a

dear and the mute tongue shout for joy. Water will gush forth in the wilderness and streams in the desert"

The Bible is God's Word manifest and abide forever. God's Word will never change or loose is Power. God will one day judge the world for its evil and unrighteousness; he will reward the righteous with

His great salvation and the redeemed will be completely saved from sin. Jesus Christ opened the eye of the man born blind during His earthly ministry and the man proclaimed and witness to the power of God and the glory of God. We must continue to pray with the Word of God in the Holy Scripture.

The Word of God or the word of the Lord refers to anything that God as spoken directly to His prophets and the people of God, beginning from Adam and Eve (Genesis 2:16-17). God spoke His word to Abraham (Genesis 12:1-3), God spoke His word to Isaac (Genesis 26:1) He spoke to Jacob (Genesis 28:13), and he spoke to Moses (Exo.3:4) God also spoke to the people of Israel from Mount Sinai when he gave Mo ses the Ten Commandments (Exo. 20:11).

God spoke through His prophets directly. The word of the Lord came to prophet Isaiah (Isa. 55:10-11) "As the rain and the snow come down from heaven and do not return to it without watering the earth and making it bud and flourish, so that it yields seed for the sower and bread for the eater, so is my word that goes out from my mouth: it will not return to me empty, but will accomplish what I desire and achieve the purpose for which I sent it."

The Word of God releases grace, power and revelation by which we as believers grow in faith and in sanctification. The Word of God has the power to impart new life make those who are spiritually dead come alive in Jesus Christ. Apostle Peter stated that "We are born again through the living and enduring Word of God (1 Peter 1:23). The Word of God causes us to grow in grace and in spiritual maturity. Peter said, "by drinking the pure mild of the Word of God, we are growing in our walk with the Lord and in salvation of our Lord."

The Word of God is the sword God has given to all the believers by which we may fight Satan (Eph. 6:17) we must remember that our Lord Jesus defeated

Satan by the Word of God during His temptations by declaring, "It is written" (Luke 4:1-11). The power of the Word of God in the scripture is incomparable we must use it in our prayers at all times (1 Peter 1:25). Peter stated that the word of the Lord stands forever this indicates that as we are on this earth, human life, human glory and all the humanities achievement are temporary and always passes away but the Word of God remains, and stands and abide forever.

When this world collapsed in its self-destruction, the Word of God will continue to endure and God will continue to judge the world by His Word on the last day. Therefore, new believers and old believers should be thirsty and earnestly long for the pure nourishment of God's Word. We should be alert and use the Word of God to clean and nourishes our soul.

5

Pray without Ceasing

1st Thessalonians 5:7-8, 16-18: "For those who sleep, sleep at night, and those who get drunk, get drunk at night. But since we belong to the day, let us be self-controlled, putting on faith and love as a breastplate, and the hope of salvation as a helmet. Be joyful always, pray continually, and give thanks in all circumstances, for this is God's will for you in Christ Jesus."

When Apostle Paul said this in the Bible—prays continually—continually does not mean to be constantly uttering formal prayers. Rather, it implies recurrent prayer. The conversation in our hearts at all times and on all occasions throughout the day must be prayer. Conversations and longings happen naturally when we focus our minds on the Lord.

Pray without ceasing: Believers must pray for everything that is going on around them, either directly to them personally or to any member of their family, they must pray for their relatives, friends, their neighbors, and for their community, city, state, and pray for the entire nation as well as pray for the schools.

We must pray for the president, the governor, and congressmen and women. We must pray for all the people in high positions in the government as well as those in lower positions and all the civil service workers in our cities, states, and the federal government sectors that are making decisions that can affect the people in the nation either positively, or negatively.

We must pray for any decision that can cut the medical aid and help services for children. We must pray for all corporations' CEOs, managers, and supervisors. We must pray for the uneasy minds

Children of God must pray in every season, and that means when it is raining, when the sun is shining, very sunny, snow is falling, when it is stormy, and in any type of weather.

Children of God must pray during emotional situations or spiritual experiences that may happen around them. They must pray for world peace, for all the nations, and where there is war or rumors of war going on, and pray for the distressed people around the world.

Pray when everything is going on great in your life and you are very happy. We must pray for the

Peace of Jerusalem because it is the city of great kings and the city of God.

We must pray continually in every situation for the unsafe among us. We must pray for the beauty of the earth, mountains, moon, sun, ocean, and everything that is in it. We must pray for the trees in the forest and the animals in the wilderness as well as all the birds that fly around the earth. We must pray for all God's creations at all times.

When we pray constantly in all seasons, we engage our hearts and minds with the good things of life. Our mind and our soul will be enriched and automatically cleared from any thought of violence, anger, evil, and all unrighteousness. We must pray without ceasing and pray continually until the gate of heaven is widely open.

6

Prayer Is God's Power Source

Prayer is God's power source. God uses our prayers to Him to do great things on this earth. Not that God cannot do it by Himself, but He wants us to pray the problem back to Him.

For example, God sent His only begotten son to the earth to redeem us from our sins not that He cannot redeem us from our sin from heaven, but the Word of God says Adam and Eve committed sin of disobedience by eating the fruit that God commanded them not to eat from the tree of knowledge of good and evil. (Genesis 2:16).

God's command was given as a test to Adam and Eve to show their love to God, as well as their belief and obedience to God. As long as Adam believed God's Word and obeyed, he was able to continue eternal life and blessed fellowship with God, until he disobey God and sin, because of Adam's sin, the curse of sin came to all God's creations including the e ntire human race that God has made in His own image.

God sent His only begotten Son to correct and redeem us from the curse of Adam sin. Death reigned from the time of Adam to the time of Moses. Jesus Christ is the second Adam and the holy Bible says (Roman 5:14-15), "Nevertheless death reigned from Adam to Moses, even over them that had not sinned after the similitude of Adam's transgression, who is the figure of him that was to come. But not as the offence, so also is the free gift, for if through the offence of one many being dead, much more the grace of God and the gift by grace, which is by one man Jesus Christ, hath abounded unto many."

The human race experienced death, because of Adam's transgression of the spoken Word of God with the death penalty. The human race was sinners by action nature and transgressors of the law that was written in their hearts and minds.

Jesus Christ came as sinless conceived by the Holy Spirit, born of the virgin many in other to redeem us from Adam's transgression of sin. The work of redemption was complete and provided by Jesus Christ through His anointment on the cross. Jesus Christ undid the effect of the fall of Adam from the Garden of Eden. This is very clear and precise action of God in the Universe.

41

Adam brought forth sin, condemnation and death to the world, Jesus Christ brought life, made us alive in God. Jesus Christ brought forth grace and truth and justification and life into human race. The work of redemption on earth brings justification to all human-kind.

Jesus Christ prays to the father on earth in order to redeem us from Adam's sin of disobedience. This should be clear to us that, if we pray we put God to work in any circumstance that is going on around us in our private life and around the world.

God will send His holy angels, the e ntire heavenly host to solve all our problems and heal all our dis- eases, quench all the fiery flame of violence, put stop to the work of evil in our lives and in our world. We must pray and our prayer must be God's power source that He can use for us and for others as well as for the people in the world.

7

Come to Him in Prayer with Confidence

C ome to Him with confidence in our prayers. God answer the prayer, pray with confidence, boldly and clearly to him. The throne of God is open when we pray with confidence, it reveal our love and dependence on God's providence and provisions.

It reveals that we know that he can do what we ask from him when we pray with confidence. It reveals our assurance, and that we are partaker in His divine knowledge and wisdom.

It reveals our sincerity, our loyalty, as a child come to the father when they are in trouble, in need, or in sickness. Believers must approach God with confidence in our prayer every time we kneel down to pray to him.

"Let us then approach the throne of grace with confidence so that we may receive mercy and find grace to help us in our time of need." (Heb. 4:16).

Jesus Christ is our high priest in heaven. We must pray with confidence.

In difficulties, prayer is the answer. In the loss of our loved ones, prayer is the answer. In our spiritual life, prayer is the answer, and in our walk with the Lord for strength, prayer is the answer.

God can do and undo in our lives. Prayer can do and undo through God when it is the prayer that God acknowledges. Dr. Reuben Archer Torrey said, "Prayer is the key that unlocks all the storehouses of God's infinite grace and power.

Bible Study International: All God is and all God has is at the disposal of prayers. Prayer can do anything God can do since God can do anything; prayer is "omnipotent." According to Charles Spurgeon's book on prayer he said, "Prayer moves the arm that moves the world."

The most important thing to know is that the more specific we are in our prayer, the quicker God is able to answer our prayer. We have to cultivate a heart of gratitude to the Lord so we will be able to receive more blessings from the Lord. God also makes our prayer lives to Him very strong. We must keep our minds positive in prayer and focus on Him confidently in our prayer.

Believers' should have an undivided prayer of one hour where the mind enters into true prayer by faith. First it takes the thought to pray. The intellect teaches us that we ought to pray. While going through this serious thinking beforehand, our mind prepares the way for true praying.

Our mind is considering what will be asking for in that hour. True praying waits till the last minute for the inspirational r e q u e s t in the hour of prayer. The mind prepares the heart beforehand as we ask for definite things from God, so beforehand the thought of prayer arises. All bad, vain, and evil thoughts are eliminated. Our minds are given over entirely to God.

Our thinking concentrates on asking of Him what we need, what we have received in the past, and what are our future requests will be. Prayer takes the total control of the believer. Prayer takes control of the body and mind during the time of prayer. It takes the whole man to embrace in its godlike sympathies the entire race of man, the sorrows, the sins, and the death of Adam's fallen race.

It takes the whole man to run parallel with God's will in saving humankind. It takes the whole man to stand with our Lord Jesus Christ as the one mediator between God and sinful man. It takes the whole man to pray until all the storms that agitate his soul and spirit are calmed down and till the stormy winds and waves cease.

It takes the whole man to pray till wicked tyrants and unjust rulers are changed in their natures, operations, lives, and governing qualities, and until they move down from their positions of power or until they stop exercising their cruel, evil power.

It requires the whole man in prayer to pray until proud, unspiritual unbelievers and sinners become gentle, lowly, and converted people. It take a whole man to pray till godliness and gravity rule in the church of Jesus Christ, in our cities, in our states, in the entire nation, in our businesses, in our homes, in public, and in our private lives.

We must make it our utmost goal to pray, and it takes all of the body of Christ to make it happen. Believers must give themselves entirely and totally to prayer. Prayer has a far-reaching effect in its influence and in its gracious effects. Prayer is an intense and profound business that deals primarily with God's plans and purposes. It takes every soul of the people of God to do it. Any half-hearted, half-minded, half-spiritual person will not get an answer to prayer.

We must be serious about knowing the importance of prayer. Prayer is a heavenly business. Our whole minds, spirits, souls, and bodies must be in the business of prayer with God. We must pray so much that our prayers will affect our characters as believers of Christ.

We must love the Lord our God with our whole hearts, souls, and minds and with our strength. Therefore, it takes entire men and women to engage in the prayer God require and that ascends straight to the throne of grace. Jesus will not take a divided heart's prayer.

The Bible says, "Blessed are they that keep His testimonies, words, and that seek Him with their whole heart." (Ps. 119:2). The book of Psalms says, "With my whole heart have I sought thee O let me not wander from thy commandments, Thy word have I hid in mine heart, that I might not sin against thee." Psalm 119:10–11.

If we keep His Word in our hearts at all times, we will be able to understand and follows His commandments with our whole heart. We will be obedient and pray effectively. The fruits of our hearts and lips will flow with prayers of thankfulness.

Our prayers will bring God down to earth. Heaven will open, and our prayers will fly to heaven if we pray with our whole hearts or pray heartedly. From the heart of man to the heart of God great things happen.

In prayer Christians are as soldiers of the Lord onward Christian soldiers fighting a life-and-death struggle. All the honor of eternal life is included in the prayer of the believer. Apostle Paul described the life of a Christian as an athlete struggling for mastery and for the crown, running a race. Everything depends on the strength that the runner puts into it. The runner should put all of his energy, concentration, determination, courage, and power into the race.

Christians put the power of their being on the race. Christians' power is quickened, strained to the very end, as our Lord said, "No man put his hands to the plough, and looking back, is fit for the kingdom of God." (Luke 9:62).

As it takes all our being to pray by pouring our hearts and minds to the Lord, so in return believers receive a great reward in answer to that prayer. All of a believer's being that he put into the true prayer, in same way all His being will receive all the blessings from God in answer to such a prayer.

This is the prayer from the heart, mind, soul, and spirit of a true, praying believer. God always makes sure that when a believer prays wholeheartedly the believer receives blessings in body, soul, and spirit.

The body is fully in good health, the food goes down to the stomach, there will be clarity of mind, right thought comes to the mind, and the mind is enlightened with more understanding of what is going on around him or her and around the world.

The believer has control of his or her thoughts, words, and deeds. Believers were blessed with divine guidance, which means God is moving and directing the mind, so they will be able to make wise decisions in everything they are doing or are going to do. All the praying ministers, pastors, and preachers of the Word of God will receive utterance to teach and preach the Word of God with clarity of tone and with the tongue of fire from the power of the Holy Spirit.

Thought flows as a stream of water from the valley. The divine power of the Holy Spirit is present with them at all times. The souls of believers will rejoice in God as they receive more benefits as the result of true prayer.

8

Boldly Approach
the Throne of Grace

Boldly approach the throne of grace. Christ as our mediator of the new covenant, our advocate we must boldly approach the throne of God of grace and great compassion.

Our Lord said, call unto me, I shall answer, before you kneel down to pray I the Lord God almighty, Father of all mercies, sustainer of all things, the creator of heaven and earth as already answer your prayer.

He said, is there anything too hard for God? No nothing is too hard for God to do, His all-powerful, and His full presence in the universe will never change. Boldly come to Him He will hear your prayer and answer your prayers. He knows the right time for everything in our lives. He knows us more than we know ourselves, and He will bring joy to our life at the blink of an eye. Come to Him boldly in your prayers.

9

Pray in the Spirit

Praying in the Spirit is different from praying with the spirit. Praying in the spirit means praying with tongues. (1 Corinthians 14:12-13), "So it is with you. Since you are eager to have spiritual gifts, try to excel in gifts that build up the church. "For this reason anyone who speaks in a tongue should pray that he may interpret what he says."

Praying in the spirit means that the Holy Spirit inspires guides, energizes, and sustains our act and words, emotions, feelings throughout our prayers. Praying in the spirit (Eph. 6:13) where we put on the armor of God in the spiritual warfare. Where we are told to be strong in the Lord and in His mighty power.

We put on the full armor of God so that we can take our stand against the devil's schemes. We were also told to take the helmet of salvation and sword of the Spirit, which is the Word of God.

Finally, we were also told that we must realized that praying with the spirit is the same as praying with the spiritual gift, which involves the human spirit as clearly different from our mind.

It should be clear to us that the Holy S pirit's activity were implied because our prayer cannot be properly ascend without the spirit power, our mind cannot depart from the Holy Spirit.

According to Paul we have our spirit and our mind praying together which means Paul pray in tongues and he also prays with foreign language or any unknown language according as the spirit gave him the utterance.

Pray at all times in the spirit. (Romans 8:9-10) "You however, are controlled not by the sinful nature but by the spirit, if the spirit of God lives in you and if anyone does not have the spirit of Christ, he does not belong to Christ. But if Christ is in you, your body is dead because of sin, yet your spirit is alive because of righteousness."

To pray in the spirit on all occasions with all kinds of prayers and supplications and request with this in mind be alert and always keep on praying for all the saints." The book of Jude also tells us (Jude vs. 25) "But you, dear friends, build yourselves up in your most holy faith and pray in the Holy Spirit.

Praying in the spirit deals with our spiritual struggling, wrestling, and battling that we believers of Jesus Christ face since after our conversion. It also builds us up for the work of the ministry, for the call of God that he called us to do for him. Building our- selves up in order to be able to help others who are babies in Christ and are still eating sold food instead of the solid Word of God.

We must build ourselves up in most holy faith, in order to live a life that is going to bring glory to His holy name, to be able to do what is going to enhance the work of the kingdom of God on earth. What is going to exult His holy name.

We must build ourselves up so that we can live a life of soul winner, a fruit bearing life, a life that is going to be one in him as he is one with the father.

The more we go through battling the more we build ourselves up by praying in the spirit, the more the spirit energizes us.

Without the indwelling power of the Holy Spirit's manifestation, revival, and awakening in our spirit soul, body we cannot live a Christian life.

In the example of Nehemiah during the exile in Babylon, he pray in the spirit and God gave him assignment to go and rebuild Jerusalem, the task was not easy but Nehemiah did it even though he battled with those who opposed him and also building himself up in the most holy faith.

One thing we need to remember is that the battle is for the Lord we have to trust him, abide in him for our victory. We must continue to pray in the spirit after one battle is won and another surface, we must pray in the spirit without ceasing.

In the New Testament, we read, living in the spirit, walking in the spirit, worshiping in the spirit, rejoicing in the spirit and praying in the spirit. These are all the activities of the Holy Spirit in the lives of the believers of Jesus Christ.

The spirit of Christ performed all these activi- ties through us and blessed us with enabling power, so that we can be able to abide in the Spirit. In the book of Acts (Acts 2:4), the apostles speak in the other languages on the day of Pentecost.

The early church believers prayed in the other languages during the worship service this continues for centuries after the apostles had martyred or died. Acts 1:8 says, "You will receive power when the Holy Spirit has come upon you." This primarily is the Spirit power in their lives so that they can be able to win sinners to the Lord.

Our action of prayer in the spirit that comes from within us the power of praying in tongues and other languages that is between us and the Lord and those that the spirit of the Lord chose to interpret.

Speaking in tongues, praying in the spirit are part of the miracle of God on the day of Pentecost during the outpouring of the Spirit of Christ. It is the part of the gift of the Holy Spirit's power for the ministry work or ministry services. "Praying with the spirit" (Romans 8:26, 27) "Likewise the Spirit helps us in our weakness; for we do not know how to pray as we ought but the spirit intercede for us." (Eph. 6:18). Pray in the Spirit at all times in every prayer and supplication.

Pray every time in the spirit. Our Lord Jesus Christ said, "that the hour is coming and it's now that those who worship the father will worship in spirit and in truth (John 4:23-24).

For the Father seeks people like this to worship him; God is a spirit those who worship him must worship him spirit and in truth."

We must worship, praise and pray to God in the spirit. (Psalm 40:5), "Many, O Lord my God are the wonders you have done. The things you planned for us no one can recount to you; were I to speak and tell of them, they would be too many to declare."

This should be the prayer of every believer. God control the timing of our lives. God has given each one of us only a short time to live on this earth; he also used our time on earth to test our faithfulness to him while living in the midst of corrupt, evil generation that opposes God and His word.

Let us use our time on earth wisely by living a life of glorification to His holy name.

10

Pray with the Spirit

Praying with the Spirit: When we pray with the indwelling Spirit of God, our mind, the spirit enlightening our heart, strengthened our weary soul energizes our spirit to pray to God on our situations and problems.

The Bible says, "Sometimes we do not know what to pray for but the spirit of God, spirit of Jesus Christ pray through us the prayer that can never be uttered."

The spirit of our Lord Jesus Christ takes total control of our prayer life, and prays for what we do not even know that we needed afar off before we know that we need that particular thing.

The spirit of the Lord, the indwelling of Christ pray for any type of sicknesses that may want to inflict us, before it happens and wash our body clean with the Word of God, and wash away our soul before the sick- ness may arrive or the sickness might not come to us at all.

If it is something that needs medical care, the Spirit of God will pray for a special doctor that will be assigned to the believer for that condition before the person step into the hospital.

The Spirit of God prays through us and solves our financial problems before it happens by sending or directing our mind to look for another job before one job ended, or fired, lay off from the present job.

Praying with the Spirit helps our prayer to get answer quicker than we thought. Because the Spirit of Jesus Christ, is the spirit of intercessor, interceding with the father at the right hand of God.

For example Hannah prays with the spirit with sorrow for being childless for a long time with her husband Elkanah. In her agony she prayed to the Lord with a fast, prayed weeping, and making her sorrowful mind known to the Lord, up to the point that Eli the prophet thought that she was drunk (1 Samuel 1:12-17), as she kept on praying to the Lord, Eli observed her mouth.

Hannah was praying in her heart, and her lips were moving but her voice was not heard. Eli thought she was drunk and said to her, "How long will you keep on getting drunk? Get rid of your wine. "Not so, my Lord." Hannah replied, "I am a woman who is deeply trouble. I have not been drinking wine or bear, I was pouring out my soul to the Lord. Do not take your servant for a wicked woman; I have been praying, here out of my great anguish and grieve. "Eli answered, "Go in peace, and May the God of Israel grant you what you have asked of him."

At that moment, Eli also interceded for Hannah by praying for her, which shows that valuable record of how important it is that all believers pray for each other. As Eli said, God of Israel granted Hannah's prayer.

The Spirit registered within her and intercede for her that her cry was heard, the sorrow of her heart was lifted up, she believed confidently that her prayer was answered the assurance of answered prayer was registered in her heart because the Spirit of God sent her prayer straight to the throne of God.

We read the Bible tells us that Hannah gave birth the following year to a son which she named Samuel and the child was dedicated to the Lord. Praying with the spirit is very important in the life of every believer of Jesus Christ.

Let us practice the habit of praying with the spirit. Holy Spirit is our helper, and he will always help us in any and all the areas of our weaknesses that we ourselves do not know.

There is a different between praying in the Spirit and praying with the Spirit. Praying in the Spirit means to pray in the Word of God, speaking forth the Word of God by the inspiration of the Holy Spirit. It entails praying with the revelation of God.

When believers receive the gift of the Holy Spirit, they will experience Christ overflowing life. The living water will flow through them from deep within the believer to other with the saving and healing power of the message of our Lord Jesus Christ.

Praying in the Spirit points to the level at which true worship and power of prayer occurs. We must come to God in complete sincerity and with a spirit that is directed by the life and activity of the Holy Spirit. Therefore, we must pray according to the truth and what is revealed to us in the holy Bible and in His Son through the Spirit.

11

Pray with Thankfulness

Prayer of thankfulness: Apostle Paul told us that in everything we are to give thanks. We must give thanks in sickness, in good health, in sorrow, in afflictions, in disappointments of life, in the morning when we wake up because in him we move, we have our being.

At night, we must give thanks for all the things good or bad that happens in the day. We must give thanks for all what we gone through in the d ay. We must learn how to give thanks for all God's provisions in our lives. We must give thanks for His mercy, love, and great compassion in our lives.

Giving God thanks every minute strengthens our relationship with him. It also makes our heart joyful every time we kneel down to pray. We must give thanks for the work of redemption. We must give thanks for what He has done for what He is doing right now in our lives and what He also continues to do in our lives. The more we give thanks the more we receive His blessings.

May our Lord and Savior Jesus Christ sanctify our hearts; make it a thankful heart for His glory from this earth to heaven. Let us gives thanks to His holy name now and forever. He is worthy, faithful, just and kind; He has given us His Son. Give thanks.

12

Pray for Your Neighbor

Pray for your neighbor. We should pray for our neighbor at all times, prayer that there should be peace between our neighbors.

As we pray this prayer frequently, a trouble or difficult neighbor will turn from bad to good, from evil to good, from hatred to love, from wickedness to good, from jealousy to love, and from violent behavior to a peaceful behavior towards us.

The more we pray for our neighbor, the more the spirit of God work with them to change their lives, so that you can live together in good harmony without problems.

It is difficult but let us learn how to pray for our neighbors because at the end when you see what God has done in the lives of your difficult, or unbelieving neighbor, you will rejoice in the Lord.

Our Lord said that we should pray for our neighbor, and the person who intentionally despises us or hates us. As we do this, the Spirit of the Lord will turn them from hatred into love, and to the love of Christ.

Pray and love your enemies. (Matthew 5:43).

13

Pray for Your Enemy with Faith

Pray with faith for your enemy. Believers' number one enemy are those who does not want, or does not want to hear the gospel or the name of Jesus Christ the son of God, or the name of God the father and the Holy Spirit.

They are violently despising Christians. Christ gave us His word and he has promised that His presence, His authority and His power will never fail us as we face all sorts of dangers.

We must let the light of our Lord shine in this world of darkness. Our Lord said (Mark 16:17-18), "And this signs will accompany those who believe: In my name they will drive out demons; they will speak in new tongues; they will pick up serpent with their hands; and when they drink deadly poison, it will not hurt them at all; they will place their hands on the sick

71

people and they will get well." Believers must bring the gospel to the lost with strong faith and with the power of prayer.

In many ways we can experience disappointment and set back in our faith formation and in the journey of faith, failures and lack of spiritual understanding at one point in our lives.

Emotional embarrassment and weaknesses, the Lord understands all what we are going through as we exercise our faith. We must be able to learn from other people who have been there before us, how they experience and exercise faith.

This will energize us and give us encouragement, knowing that great people in the Bible experience failures, sins, and disappointment; even in their weaknesses, they continued to trust God and continue to have strong faith in him.

We should follow their steps in whatever we are going through, we must continue to focus on the Lord obey, trust and walk with him by faith. The Bible said Abraham believed God; he was called a friend of God.

Abraham was known for His strong faith and His fellowship with God. The Bible says (Heb. 11: 8-11, 17), "By faith Abraham, when called to go to a place he would later receive as inheritance, obeyed and went, even though he did not know where he was going.

By faith, he made His home in the Promised Land like a stranger in a foreign country, he lived in tents, as did Isaac and Jacob, who were heirs with him of the same promise." Abraham's faith grows after he was called by God.

Abraham disobey God's plan for himself and travel to Egypt, he listened to Sarah his wife, and have a child with his house made Hagar without waiting for the promise of God. (Genesis 12, 16, 17, 20, 21). Abraham's faith took years to develop but his love for God did not change.

Finally, Abraham got to the point where he surrendered everything to God; his will, emotions, plans, ability. He trusted God to the point that he was willing to sacrifice Isaac his son on the altar to God.

Abraham did not step back or run away from his call of God. Even though he went through many, many difficulties. God continues to show His great love and faithfulness to Abraham his trust for grew as a child trust his earthly father, he trusted God more and more every day.

The life of Abraham should teach all the believers that we should love the Lord more and more every day of our lives. We should not allow our failures to move us away from God's plans for our life, or interfere with our fellowship, relationship with the Almighty God.

If anything makes us fall into sin, we should pray for forgiveness and restoration and back into the presence and into His light where darkness cannot over power us. We should continue to pray for God's power source of strength in our faith walk with God. We must believe in the existence of a personal, infinite, holy God who cares for us.

We must also believe that God reward us when we earnestly seeking His face, knowing that our reward is the joy of finding him and enjoying His full presence now and forever. He is our shield, deliverer and our strong tower, our great reward, our fortress, and our life.

Abraham's faith is an example for all the believers for all God's people; we are on the journey of faith in this world, traveling to God's holy city of Jerusalem, which is in heaven. If we pray for our enemy by faith, God will turn them to be the seeker of God. Our Lord said pray for your enemy.

We must pray for our enemy at all times. Our Lord Jesus said love your enemy (Luke 6:27-28), "But I tell you who hear me; love your enemy, and do good to those who hate you, bless those who curse you." Our Lord Jesus tells how we are to live with other people with peace. We are the member, part of His body.

Christ is the mediator of a new covenant. We are obligated as part of His body to follow the demands and the teaching that our Lord set for us. Loving our enemies mean, we must exercise a sincere concern for their good and well-being, we must try to reach them with salvation if it is possible, or there is a room to

Introduce the gospel to them. Since we know that the unsaved are in need of salvation.

If they have salvation, God indwelling Holy Spirit is in them, they will not be our enemy. Therefore, we must try our best no matter how upset we are, after praying for them earnestly to change from being our enemy to our friend.

We know that this people are hostile to God and His people, we must pray that the power of the love of God fall upon them, by repaying them with good for their evil, they might receive the resurrected Christ's love and the faith of the gospel of God.

Loving our enemy does not mean that we should let the evildoers continue their wickedness. We must give honor to God and seek the safety and goodness of other people around us action must be taken that will put stop to the work of evil people physically, spiritually according to the law of individual country.

Let us pray for our enemies and the enemies of the cross of Christ. There are some enemies of the cross of Christ these enemies are professed believers who were corrupting the gospel of God by immoral lives with false teaching.

We must pray for them that the truth of the gospel be open to them, that the Holy Spirit's illuminating light penetrates through their heart and mind, and they will lovingly preach the true gospel.

14

Pray for the Body of Christ on Earth

We must pray for the body of Christ in all the nations. Apostle Paul says pray for me: "Pray also for me, that whenever I open my mouth, words may be given me so that I will fearlessly make known the mystery of the gospel, for which I am ambassador in chains, pray that I may declare it fearlessly, as I should." (Eph. 16: 19-20).

We must learn how to pray for all the believers of Jesus Christ, for pastors, elders, deacons, and all the staffs in the ministry, that our Lord will make them faithful in their service of the Lord, that they will not fall into temptation such as embezzling the church funds and fall into any form of sexual immoralities. We must pray effectively.

God on behalf of all the believers such as our husband, wife, children, all believers, and missionaries. We must pray for God's will to be done in their lives, blessing of spiritual wisdom, blessing of living holy lives that will be pleasing to the Lord Jesus Christ.

Prayer that they should be a fruit bearer for the kingdom of Jesus Christ, we must pray for all the believers to be spiritually strengthened by the power of the Holy Spirit, we must pray that their faith, love, and righteousness grow more and more in the Lord.

We must pray for all the body of Christ to give God the father, God the Son, and God the Holy Spirit great and unceasing thankfulness every day with joy.

Our prayer is to continue living in hope of heaven, the realization awareness that heaven is our home we sojourn on this earth temporarily Christ is our hope of glory.

We must pray that all the body of Christ get closer to Him every day and maintained intimate relationship with Him personal relationship with Him, and to be one in him as Christ is one with the father.

We must pray that the great commission be fulfilled through all the believers on this earth to the point that they will take the gospel of God to where the gospel has never been heard before in the language of that town or that village.

We must pray that the body of Christ be filled with Jesus Christ's revelation and love; we must pray that all the body of Christ, all the believers to be complete in Christ and in the fullness of God the father Almighty.

We must pray without ceasing for all the body of Christ, household of faith and believers to learn how to show kindness to others and especially to the sinners and the lost.

Our Lord said we are the salt of the earth, as a salt is valuable to give flavor to preserve from decay or corruption; we believers must be a Godly example in the world and must resist moral decay, corruption, violent, jealousy in our society in the community, city, and state and in our country.

We must pray for God's kingdom on earth now with the fulfillment of His future return and the establishment of God's eternal kingdom of the new heaven and the new earth where only righteousness dwells.

We must pray for all the believers that they received the spirit's discernment, to be able to discern evil things and good things, to be able to discern the spirit of error from the spirit of truth, or the true Holy Spirit.

We must pray that all the believers live sincere lives blameless in the eye of man and God. To be able to live a life that is worthy of His calling.

We must pray that all the body of Christ were delivered from the power of sin and death. "Apostle Paul reminded the people to be subject to rulers and authorities, to be obedient, to be ready to do whatever is good, to slander no on e to b e peaceable and considerate, and to show true humility toward all men." (Titus 3:12).

It is very important for our witnesses and for the furtherance of the gospel, that believers must be obedient t o the government authorities, they must obey the civil law, to be a good citizens and to live a peaceful and respectable lives with their neighbors as long as the governmental law does not cause a conflicting factors with our commitment to the Lord.

15

Pray for the Peace of Nations

Pray for the peace of all the nations on earth. We must pray for the peace in all the nation of earth without ceasing or every day, when the nation is at war with one another because of wrong doing of few people, the people of both nations, the two nations suffer.

The people who suffered more are the children of both nations, they could be killed have no food, lost their father or mother or both parents during the war.

Therefore, these innocent children are paying for practically what they don't know anything about at the beginning of their lives. Prayer is needed every day for all the nation of earth.

The second people that suffered during the war of one country to another are women. Women suffered the loss of their husband. Boyfriends, they were opened to torture such as rape, and women trafficking all over the world. We all the body of Christ must pray without ceasing for our young college students, and senior citizens during the war of nations.

The third people who suffered and live in pain some times for the rest of their lives are the parents and relatives who lost their loved ones during the war.

We must pray for these people; they need our prayers to continue their lives. We must pray for the government officials, presidents, governors, and other high-ranking government officials to continue making decisions that will bring peace and stability to their country instead of war.

These people needs our prayers because the country could be 800 million in population but few people will make a decision that will turn the lives of the rest 750 million upside down sorrows flows through the hearts of every one. Unrest of mind and fears prevail.

The psalmist told us in (Psalm 122:6-7), "Pray for the peace of Jerusalem: may those who love you be secure. May there be peace within your walls and security within your citadels." Therefore, we should pray for the peace of all the nations.

In 1 Timothy 2:8, we are told, "I want men everywhere to lift up holy hands in prayers without anger or disputing."

It is very important for all the believers to lift their hands and offer prayers aloud especially when we are praying in a public place for the nations; for our prayers to be effective, we must pray wholeheartedly for our prayer to be effective, we must pray with clean hearts, mind, make ourselves holy and live righteous lives.

As believers and children of God, we must show concern for all God's people peaceful lives in all the nations.

We must pray for our leaders that they will search for the truth in everything, every situation, and every decision making and embrace, hold to wh a is right and justified.

We must pray for our leaders, and leaders of the nations for the Lord to give them courage and self-control to stay away from what is false foolish and untrue, because without restraint without leadership, we will be blind and deaf to the truth.

We must pray that the Lord Jesus Christ build the manner of those who are in authority with the power of the Holy Spirit so that they can have Christ like character such as integrity, value and boldness to bring forth justice that is based on the truth.

They must love the truth more than power. The value the purpose of their service to the world they should remember that God call them to be the leader of the truth. We must pray for people in all several of businesses in this world.

We must pray that the name of Jesus Christ be honored in every place of business. For our Lord to bless all that expresses His kingdom that people in prisons will hear the gospel of God preach to them, so that they can follow Jesus Chris for their salvation, worship him and fellowship with him.

We must pray that the prisoner would be protected from other violent prisoners, that they serve their time in peace and be released from the prisons on time with a new life full of strength, wisdom and knowledge to live the rest of their lives for Christ. We must pray that God imparted them with a new life.

16

Pray for the Sinner
and the Lost

We should pray for the sinners and the lost. Our Lord said (Luke 19:9-10), "Today salvation has come to this house, because this man, too, is a son of Abraham. For the son of man came to seek and to save what was lost."

This statement is the key to our Lord Jesus' reason for coming to the earth, and is the main idea of the message of the gospel; it points to the heart of our Lord Jesus Christ's earthly mission. This statement is the central and the depth of our mission on earth as the followers of Jesus.

Christ's work of saving the lost was continuing up until few days before His crucifixion. In the house of Zacchaeus the tax collector the people of Jesus days hate the tax collectors; they do not want to have anything to do with them. Because tax collectors earning and making money by collecting more than they should from the people, people despised them. Jesus was concern for the soul of Zachaeus.

Jesus expects the same from us today; to take the gospel to rejected, poor despised people in our society, to the prisoners in the nations, to the wicked people to the Idol worshipers, Muslims, Hindus, Buddhists, atheists, the homeless, and the richest person on earth.

We must reach the lost for Christ for whom He died and rose again from the grave, so that they might be saved and receive eternal life—life everlasting. He saved the thief on His right hand on the day of His crucifixion, that means Jesus work until the last minute before He died on the cross.

Our Lord also said, "As the Father sent me I have sent you." He gave us the great commissions which must be fulfill by all the body of Christ through the power of the indwelling of the Holy Spirit.

The Holy Bible (John 3:16), "For God so loved the world, that he gave His only begotten son, that whosoever believeth in him should not perish, but have everlasting life."

17

The Power of Prayer

We believers of Jesus Christ should not at any time, in any situation and circumstances under estimated the power of prayer. Prophet Elijah prayed that it would not rain for three years God answered his prayer and he prayed again. God opens the heavens and the rain falls to the land (1 Kings 17:1) "As the Lord the God of Israel lives, whom I serve, there will be neither dew nor rain in the next few years except at my word."

Elijah prays powerfully and he declared his power of prayer that was given him by God because the people of his days worship the idol of Baal. He was commissioned to awake and warn the Israelites and call them back to the God of Israel. What happened is that Elijah had strong relationship and unceasing devotion to God—His covenant, his faith, courage, and loyalty to God helped him to strongly oppose the idol worshipers of Baal.

On one occasion, Elijah's powerful prayer was heard from heaven, God sent fire from heaven to consume the sacrifice. (1 Kings 18:38) "Then the fire of the Lord fell and burned up the sacrifice, the wood, the stones and the soil and also licked up the water in the trench."

This miracle performed by Prophet Elijah commissioned him as God's prophet and it was also proved that Israel's God alone was the one and only the living God whom only they should pray to, serve, and worship.

It is the same today and forever, we believers of Jesus Christ our Savior should only for the manifestation of God's spirit and power to be bestow upon us. We should be able to pray to God with the power of prayer.

We should be able to expresses our faith and receive supernatural victory in answer to prayer. Believers should be able to face the false preachers, pastors of our days with the power of prayer and expose them so people will not be joining them, thinking that their true servant of the Lord or true pastor, or minister of the Word of God.

Elijah prayed powerfully (Verses 17-21) "The son of the woman that Elijah was staying with was sick, he grew worse and worse, and finally the child stopped breathing" Elijah called and prayed powerfully to God, God restored the life of the boy in answer to Elijah's power of prayer.

The Lord heard Elijah's cry for help, same thing today believers must cry to the Lord in all our problems and we will receive answer to our prayers. The prayer of a righteous man is powerful it bring them nearer and nearer to God, it open many doors of life opportunities and a way to spirit filled and control life, bring joy, provide, blesses them with power for minis try.

Power of prayer build up Christians in their daily devotion to the Lord and also build them up spiritually, increase their faith and make them strong give believers deeper insight into Christ's provisions for victorious living. The power of prayer is not based on the individual who is praying but the power of prayer is from God whom we direct our prayers.

Our passion behind the prayers, or the purpose of our prayer is very important as well as the tools that are used for answering all prayers that are in agreement with His will. God's answers are always yes, if it is in our best interest and is according to His will for our life.

When our heart's desires are the same with His will, we must be confident that our prayers have been answered. The power of prayer brings glory, honor, and might to the presence of God in the world.

The Spirit of God holds and sustains the earth through the power of prayers of every people on earth. We should continue to pray, maintain a close relationship with the Lord communion with the Father through the Son with the power of the Holy Spirit.

Whether it is a prayer of petition to God, worship, prayer of repentance, prayer of praises, or prayer of thanksgiving coming from our hearts, God wants all the believers to pray to him, He knows our hearts and minds, we must commune with Him in prayers every day, we must all pray for the power of prayer by praying for one another for healing, financial stability, death, disappointments, and other in any kinds of adversities that plagued the world of sin.

We must be clear and precise in our power of prayer the Word of God is full of so many accounts of the power of prayer, power of prayer overcome the strong hold of the enemies' attack physically and spiritually, power of prayer has conquered sin and death (2 Kings 4:3-36). Power of prayers has brought healing to many people who are suffering from different kinds of illness.

The power of prayer also grants us great wisdom knowledge and understanding in various situations in the world. (James 5:13-15) "Is any one of you in trouble? He should pray. Is anyone happy? Let him sing songs of praise. Is any one of you sick? He should call the elders of the church to pray over him and anoint him with oil in the name of the Lord. And the prayer offered in faith will make the sick person well; the Lord will raise him up."

Believers who are going through distress, poverty and many diverse troubles should seek for strength from God through the power of prayer. They should draw near, call onto the mediator of a new covenant Jesus Christ, who is also our advocate between man and God, advocate of a new covenant.

He will present our case before God because he was sitting right there at the right hand of God. Making intercession for you and me. Given us mercy and grace to help in all the areas of our time of need. (Heb. 4:16) Believers must cast all cares upon him because he cares for us.

We should take the Word of God seriously, by expressing our joy, singing songs of joy and praises to him. When our prayers are offered with faith, it will help and make the sick people or person get well.

Either physically, mentally, or emotionally by asking for prayers of the elders and leaders of the church, even though we all know that this is one of the responsibility of an elder in the church is to pray the prayer of faith for the sick people, members of the church and those who call from outside the church for prayer.

The oil will present the healing offered by faith will make the sick person through the power of the holy spirit James told us that effective prayers must be offered in faith if the sick are to be healed. The power of prayer is so great in the lives of believers because Jesus will do immeasurably, exceedingly, abundantly more than what we ask in prayer if we pray powerfully to him. It brings God close to us so that we can listen and hear His directions for our life.

18

The Soul and Mind of Prayer

Soul and mind of prayer: We must concentrate fully on our Lord and Savior, by taken our minds away from whom we are, take our mind away from friends, children, relatives, parents, husband, we must take our mind away from our problems, difficulties, afflictions, tribulations and looking unto Jesus the author and finisher of our faith by this we will get hold of power of prayer that can move the mountain.

We need to focus on Jesus, what he has done in our lives, what he is presently doing in our lives, and what is His will for us in the future.

We need to wake up every morning with the power of indwelling of the Holy Spirit calling him in our morning prayer to direct, and guide, control of our daily business in our offices, establishment, in our own business, control our spending habit our medical appointments, and all our engagements. Our trust in the Lord will bring us top great victory and blesses us with the power of prayer we needed to live strong, peaceful lives.

God's Word is a food for our soul we must let the truth of the Word of God stay in our hearts at all times. We mu st see the Word of God as we drink water, breath in air, and as eating food.

All these three essential things we cannot do without on daily basis, therefore, if we put a verse of the Word of God in our heart every day, we will be so powerful in our prayers than what we can imagine.

Our faith will increase, our strength grows, and we just name it, and claim it from the Lord if he knows that what we ask for is good for us.

The most important thing for us to know is that the spirit of our Lord and Savior Jesus Christ will be so active in our lives and in the lives of those who close to us. If they were going through life obstacles, you will just pray for them and God will answer the prayer.

We must read the Scriptures, stay in the Word every day until the word comes alive and abides with us and in us.

Through the power of the Holy Spirit. We will find out that there will be no room to think negatively or give room to any negative thought to come across our mind. You will think good, and feel good emotionally, and there will be no room for sadness, fear, anger, and any other thought that troubles the human mind.

The light of the Lord will continue to shine upon you wherever you go, in whatever you are doing, your heart will be full of illuminating light of the Holy Spirit you will be complete and be a clean vessel that God can use to help others just has he used Isaiah put his mind and soul on prayer that God was so happy with him up to the point that he allowed him to see all the coming events in God's plan of salvation through his day to day communion with God.

Isaiah 6:1-9 tells us about Isaiah's personal relationship with the Lord, he came to understand the call of God in his life, "woe to me" I cried. "I am ruined" for I am a man of unclean lips, and I live among a people of unclean lips, and my eyes have seen the King, the Lord Almighty. (vs. 8) "Then I heard the voice of the Lord saying, "Whom shall I send? And who will go for us? And I said, "Here am I send me."

Isaiah stayed close to the Lord through his prayer and supplications and reading of the Word of God, until he was close enough to receive cleansing from the Lord and he was commissioned as a prophet to deliver the message of God to the people of God of his days. During our Lord's ascension He gave us the great commission to proclaim the gospel of God's salvation to all the people in all the nations. (Matt. 28:18-20).

We must pray and read the Word of God daily in order for our Lord and Savior to be able to send us to the end of the earth. We will be able to answer our calling to the mission's field, ministerial services just as Isaiah respond with great joy and said, "Here am I. Send me."

Another model of soul and mind of prayer was by prophet Jeremiah. Jeremiah was called by God to be a prophet. (Jeremiah 1:5-9) He prayed day and night, he read the Word of God every day, he maintained close and personal relationship with the Almighty God to the point that one day God called him "Before I formed you in the womb I knew you, before you were born I set you apart, I appointed you as a prophet to the nations" (vs. 10) "The Lord reached out his hand touched my mouth and said to me, "Now, I have put my words in your mouth see, today I appoint you over nations and kingdoms to uproot and tear down, to destroy and overthrow, to build and to plant."

In this story, God assured Jeremiah that his message would be fulfilled by him and his words would be God's Words, Jeremiah was commissioned to be an ambassador and representative of God the nations. Because God put His words on Jeremiah's mouth whenever Jeremiah speaks the spirit of God spoke through him from the reigns of King Josiah to Zedekiah Jeremiah's messages contained the elements of judgment and restoration.

An example of soul and mind of prayer is Apostle Paul after his conversion on the road to Damascus. (Acts 9:3-11) Saul was praying with his mind and soul in Damascus where he was staying. The prayer was so powerful coming out of his mind and soul to the point that he was clean and clear enough that our Lord heard his prayer and sent Ananias. "Go to the house of Judas on Straight Street and ask for a man from Tarsus named Saul, for he is praying."

Paul after his conversion he immediately obey the word of the Lord, he answered the call of the Lord to be his witness and bring great commission of the gospel to the gentiles.

Paul committed himself to prayer and fasting for three days by the time Ananias arrived to Paul's place, to lay hands on him, he realized that Paul has been fully converted and is ready to serve the Lord as other disciple of Jesus Christ and was ready to fulfill God's commission, and he only need to be baptized to show as prove of identification with Christ openly and publicly. Paul has his sight restored and he was filled with the power of indwelling of the Holy Spirit.

Paul accepted our Lord Jesus as the one and only the Messiah, because he pray with his mind and soul and he was fasting for three days and three nights with power to the Lord with deeper and deeper commitment to the Lord. The same thing could happen to all the believers of Jesus today if after our conversion we engage in a continuous prayer with our mind and soul.

We will be able to receive all the necessary and be able to fulfill this great commission that he assigned for us immediately after our conversion, we will be able to be receive the power of the Spirit and have such a tremendous spiritual hunger and thirsty, longing to know Jesus and the power of His resurrection, get closer and closer to him through prayer and fasting which will help us to receive revelations upon revelations about the things around us now and things to come, and thing that will happen to us, to others, to the entire nation, and all the nation of the world.

We will be able to live a wholeness lives separated from sin and sanctified by the Holy Spirit. Helping other to turn to the Lord for the strength and joy to live a life that is well pleasing in His sight, a life of calling the lost to him. May the Lord help us in this desire to serve and have unconditional love for Him. Jesus is calling us to put our soul and mind in our prayers.

19

The Result of Prayer

The result of prayer happens the moment we pray, we should be able to thank God for our prayers because He know that you ask according to His will.

Your prayer and petition are presented to the Lord in submission, confidence and trust in accordance to the father's will as revealed in the Word of God or by the Holy Spirit.

All God's will is revealed in the scriptures, He gave His word for our guidance, protection, provisions and for all our needs.

As we seek His will for our daily lives, He is faithful and just to fulfill our needs according to His riches in glory, (Philippians 4:19) "My God will meet all your needs according to His glorious riches in Christ Jesus."

Paul is assuring us that God will meet all our needs. Paul emphasizes the loving care of God the

Father for His children. He is our heavenly Father. He will meet all our needs physically, materially, medically and spiritually as we cast all our needs upon him. He will meet all our needs in Christ Jesus the mediator and our advocate.

Union with Christ and in His fellowship we can experience God's love and provision. God will answer our prayers because he cares for His children. The result of prayer also shapes, turns, and blesses us with the spirit of humility. In (1 Peter 1:2) "who have been chosen according to the foreknowledge of God the father, through the sanctifying work of Spirit, for obedience of Jesus Christ and sprinkling by His blood."

We must see the result of our prayer to the father because we have been chosen according to the foreknowledge of God to be God's people according to God's own comprehensive knowledge of His plan of redemption in Christ even before the foundation of the universe according to God's eternal love.

All believers must know and respond in faith through their prayers. (1 Peter 5:5) We are called to humble ourselves as the children of God. "Young men, in the same way are submissive to those who are older. All of you, clothe yourselves with humility toward one another, because, God opposes the proud but gives graces to the humble." Humility is achieved by one of the results of prayer. Humility should be a special gift for all God's people.

It means we must put all our pride down, the more we pray the more the holy spirit uses our prayer to humble us in the area of our life that we are too proud, all we think we are the one that made us what we are yesterday and today. Believers must develop honest awareness of our weaknesses, we should give God the praises and credit for accomplishments and achievements in our lives.

When we stay in the Word of God, and pray without ceasing we are doing what Peter exults us to do tie ourselves with clothe of humility in order to be identified as believers in Christ, and we will receive God's grace in all our needs. We will be able to see clearly that God cares for every one of His children, which he emphasized in His word. Once we give him all our troubles the result of our prayer is the spirit of humility take control of our hearts, mind and soul.

20

The Answer to Prayers

Our answers the prayers will be so overwhelmed and so magnificent that we will not be able to comprehend it. (Philippians 4:13) "I can do everything through him who gives me strength."

Believers must know that Christ's power and grace is so great it enables us to do so many thing and all the things that he asked us to do.

In the Old Testament, God revealed himself as God of Grace, He showed His love to the people of Israel and to the entire world, not because we deserve His grace and love, but because God is a great God, it is in His attribute of desire to be faithful to the covenant of His promises made to Abraham, Isaac, and Jacob.

God is the God of justice given to us what we deserve; God is the God of mercy and He spared us from what we deserve; God is the God of grace, He gave us what we do not deserve, the Bible says for God so loved the world that He gave His only begotten Son (John 3:16) God's grace is the giving of His Son to us sinners.

His grace multiplied to the believer through the power of the Holy Spirit, imparting forgiveness, a new life, acceptance of Christ redemptive work of salvation, and power to do God's will. Christianity is based on God's grace. He save us "Not of righteousness which we have done, but according to His mercy he saved us, by the washing of regeneration, and renewing of the holy spirit, no one should boast it is the gift of God."

(Titus 3:4-7) "But when the kindness and love of God our Savior appeared, he saved us, not because of righteous things we had done, but because of His mercy.

He saved us through the washing of rebirth and renewal by the Holy Spirit, whom he poured out on us generously, through Jesus Christ our Savior, so that having been justified by His grace, we might become heirs having the hope of eternal life."

The washing means the life of the believers Christ life through the baptism Renewal by the Holy Spirit means that believers were imparted Christ life to the believers as they gave their lives completely to God through Jesus Christ His Son.

Our prayer will be constantly be answered because the Holy Spirit's work which include baptizing the believers just as the day of Pentecost which still continue up until today. God always supplies us with abundant grace and power as a result of our new life in Christ. With this in mind, believers received an automatic answer to their prayers through the gift of grace and a new life in Christ.

The Holy Spirit who indwells the believers is the spirit of Christ because it is Christ who imparts the spirit to the believers at conversion also baptizes believers with the spirit, the same spirit that empowered and anointed Jesus during His earthly ministry and His redemptive mission.

Once believers stand firm in one spirit, the unity of the spirit consists living a life that is worthy of him, standing complete and firm in one spirit and purpose, striving to please him in all that I do, always ready to defend the gospel truth according to the revelation, and against those who are the enemies of the cross of Jesus Christ living in the unity of the spirit at the bond of peace. Believers' answers to prayers are unlimited, immeasurable, amazing, and marvelous.

Let us pray to the one from whom all the blessings flow, all the keys to life and godliness is in His hands. Let us pray to God our maker, the ruler of our soul the only one who have unconditional love for us, who listen to prayers and answers prayers according to our best interest and as well as according to His divine will for us. Let us pray. He is waiting to hear from us.

"As the father has loved me, so I have loved you. Continue ye in my love." (John 15:9). The secret of answered to prayer is to remain in Christ. The more intimate our life in Christ through prayer the more our prayers will be answered.

Our Lord calls believers to a life of intimacy and personal relationship that leads to full devotion to him. The more we will be strengthened the more our prayers will be answered the more souls will be won; sinners will be automatically converted when they see the great things that is happening in our life.

Let us pray to our heavenly father through Jesus Christ our Lord. (Luke 11:5-8). Our lord teaches us about the importunity prayer: "Suppose one of you has a friend and he goes to him at midnight and says, friend, lend me three loaves of bread, because a friend of mine on a journey has come to me, and I have nothing to set before him (vs. 8). I tell you the truth, he will not get up and give him the bread because he is his friend, yet because of the man's boldness he will get up and give him as much as he needs."

Believers must pray with persistence, confidently, clearly, again and again until the answer to their prayer comes. We must not give up in our prayer request, if we know that it is something that we really need and is according to the will of God, something that will better our lives, something that will give peace and tranquility, something that will help us to enhance His

Kingdom on earth, something that will elevate us physically, spiritually we must continue to ask, seek, and knock for it, until God answers that prayer.

Boldly let Him know that this is an urgent request, "Lord, I need You in this particular situation." (James 1:5-8) "If any of you lack wisdom, he should ask God, who gives generously to all without finding fault, and it will be given to him. But when he asks, he must believe and not doubt, because he who doubts is like a wave of the sea, blown and tossed by the wind. That man should not think he will receive anything from the Lord; he is double minded man, unstable in all he does."

Believers were told if they lack wisdom to ask God for wisdom so that they can be able to coop with all the trials of life and they can be deliver from all those trials. Wisdom that James was talking about is a spiritual wisdom that will give the believer the ability to see what they are going through at the same time, evaluate life as conducted from God's perspectives.

It will help the believer to be able to discern each situation and make the right choices, doing the right things making progress in all the areas of their lives in accord to the revealed God's Word and leading of the Holy Spirit.

Believers will receive great wisdom to live a life of peace in this world of hatred, evil, violence, and wickedness by coming to God, asking for wisdom by faith. We will be able to endure any trials with great wisdom and with faith. Another important aspect of prayer is that believer's prayers must be back up with the scriptures.

Summary

Christ ignites the hearts by the Word of God with passionate hope. Christ opens the eye of those who are born blind by not knowing the Word of God, or have never heard the Word of God spoken to them so that they can be able to recognize the risen Lord and Savior Jesus Christ.

When the eye of their heart opens and Jesus Christ reveal himself to us, imparted our hearts with the blazing and fire of the Word of God, a new heart and new life begins and we develop strong hope in His Word.

As He opened the eye of the two people traveling on the road to Emmaus and also explained the scripture to them. "Then their eyes were opened and they recognized him and he disappeared from their sight."

And they said, "Were not our hearts burning within us while he talked with us on the road and opened the scriptures to us." (Luke 24: 31-32). What an amazing joy that day may be in the life of newly converted believers of Jesus Christ when the scripture will be open to them beginning from the Old Testament to the New Testament.

Let us pray: Lord Jesus Christ let all the people of this universe seek thee and find thee. Father, Son, and Holy Spirit, let them be able to give thee honor, glory, blessings and praises that due you Oh, Lord.

Let all the soul of human being be able to honor thee in faithfulness, great wisdom, truth, love and power. In thy precious, powerful, great and mighty holy name, a name above all names I pray, Amen, Amen, Amen.

"Pray always." (1 Thes. 5: 17). What else does this simple scriptural sentence mean except that all our lives God call us to prayer?

Praying is not easy. Every day so many other things call for attention. And the world around us puts little value on prayer; it tells us to put our minds to more important matters. It is not easy to pray today.

Yet, God tells us to pray.

Beginning and ending the day are privileged moments for prayer. These morning and evening prayers drawn from the psalms and the scriptures also include selections from the Word of God. During the Advent, Christmas, and Lenten season, which are the great seasons of prayer for the Church, you will find special resources at this website.

As you use this site, may the Holy Spirit within you come to your aid and guide you gently to the God who loves you.

Bibliography

Baillie, John, the Interpretation of Religion: An Introductory Study of Theological Principles. Edinburgh, UK: Charles Scribner's Sons, 1928.

Bultmann, Rudolf, Jesus and the Word. London: Deutsche Bibliotheca, 1926.

J. Julius Scott, Jr., The Substructure of New Testament Theology. Portland, OR USA: James Nisbet & Co., Ltd, 1952.

Ernest De Witt Burton, The Present Task in New Testament Studies. University of Chicago Press, Cambridge, UK: Cambridge University Press, 1936

Ralph Earle, Th.D., Editor, Harvey J. S. Blaney, Th.M. Carl Hanson, Th.D., USA Exploring The New Testament Beacon Hill Press Kansas City, MO, USA.

Walter Brueggema, The Theology of the Old Testament, Eng. tr. New York: Harper & Brothers, 1958 Westminster John Know Press, 2001.

Kenneth Wuest, The New Testament an Expanded Translation. Wm. B. Eerdmans Publishing Company, Grand Rapids, MI, USA.

E. F. Scott, Hendrickson Publisher, Inc., T. & T. Publisher New York, NY USA The Fourth Gospel Its Purpose and Theology. T. & T. Clark, 1906.

James D. Smart, The Interpretation of Scripture The Westminster Press Philadelphia, PA, USA, 1958.

The Holistic Hardware Bible, Biblical Tools for Building Lives.

Biblical Index

References to prayer in the Scriptures, where people in the Old Testament and in the New Testament pray powerfully and receive answers to their prayers.

Genesis 1:1, 2:16–17, 28:13, 26:1, 12:1–3, 2:16, 12,16, 17

Exodus 20:11, 3:4

1 Samuel 1:12–17

1 Kings 17:1, 18:38, 17–21

2 Kings 4:3–36

Psalm 119:2

Psalm 119:10–11

Psalm 40:5, 122:6–7

Psalm 40:5, 122:6–7

Isaiah 62:5, 55:11, 35:1–6, 55:10–11, 6:1–9

Jeremiah 32:41

Lamentations 3:22-23

Matthew 21:21–22, 6:5–14, 5:43, 28:18–20

Mark 16:17–18

Luke 11:1–13, 15:11–21, 17–19, 11:9–10, 4:1–11,
  6:27–28, 19:9–10, 11:5–8, 24:31–32

John 3:16, 15:1–7, 13:3–8, 4:23–24, 15:9

Acts 2:4, 1:8, 9:3–11

Romans 8:9-10, 8:26

1 Corinthians 14:12–13

Ephesians 6:18, 6:17, 6:13, 6:19–20

Philippians 4:6–7, 4:19, 4:13

1 Timothy 2:8

Titus 3:12, 3:4–7

Hebrews 4:16, 11:8–11, 17

James 5:13–15, 1:5–8, 5:13–15, 1:5–8

1 Peter 1:23, 1:25, 1:2, 5:5

1 John 3:18–22

Jude vs. 20

Benediction

66 The grace of our Lord Jesus Christ, the love of God, and the communion of the Holy Ghost, be with you all." 2 Cor. 13:14.

Amen, amen, amen.

MAY GOD BE GLORIFIED FOR THE GREAT THINGS HE HAS DONE IN OUR WORLD.

Books previously
Published by the author
Grace Dola Balogun by
Grace Religious Books Publishing
& Distributors, Inc.

**PRAYER THE SOURCE OF STRENGTH
FOR LIFE – English Edition**

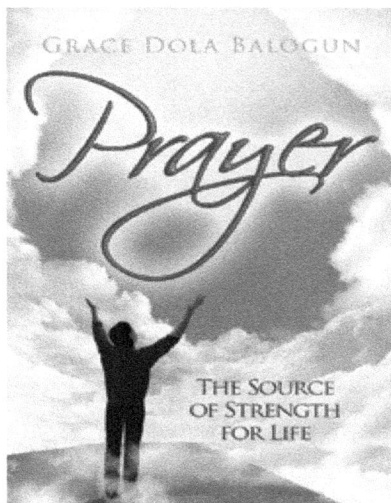

Prayer the Source of Strength for Life is a powerful book that will energize your spirit to pray more and more until the prayer is part of your life and until the gate of heaven is opened and your prayer is answered. Your prayer life will change your life.

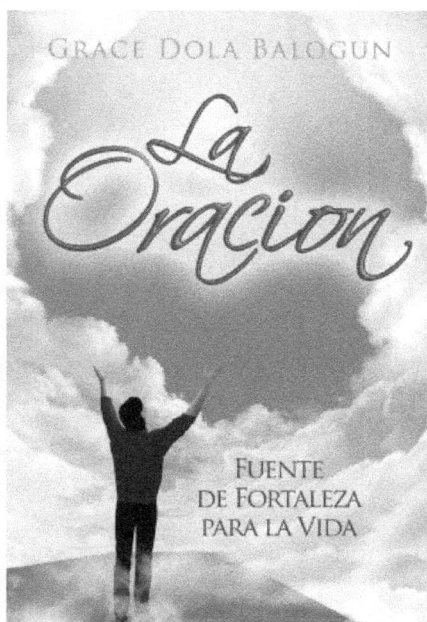

LA ORACION FUENTE DE FORTALEZA PARA LA VIDA – Spanish Edition.

Dios nos dio el poder de la oracion, quiere que lo usemos; debemos illamar, comunicarnos con el en todo lo que estemos pasando. El espera saber de nosotros.

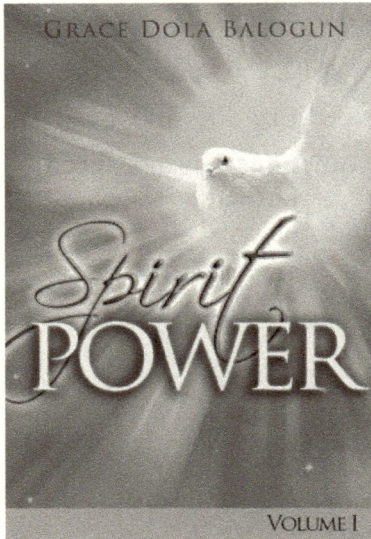

Spirit Power Volume I and II both discuss the power of the Holy Spirit in the life of believers

The Power of the Spirit of God begins from the creation of the world up until today. That power will also continue until Christ returns to reign. Hallelujah!

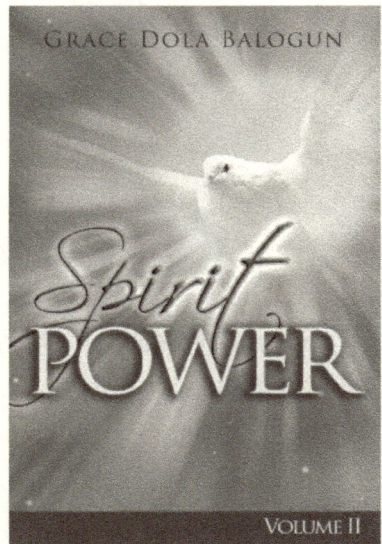

THE CROSS AND THE CRUCIFIXION

Our Lord Jesus Christ died on the Cross to bring forth love and compassion. Sin's impact on human life brings all other evil into our world, from one society to another society, from one culture to another.

But in Christ, we are clothed with His holiness. We have the gift of eternal life. The gate of heaven is open and we are eligible for our inheritance in heaven.

Hallelujah! Hosanna in the Highest. Jesus Christ paid it all, unto Him all we owe. The Cross of Christ is the Cross of joy, peace, and righteousness to all who believe in Him.

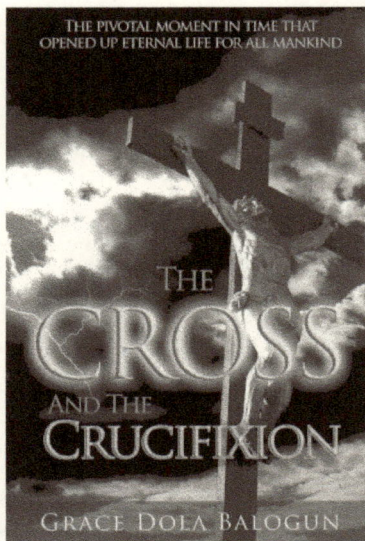

THE PIVOTAL MOMENT IN TIME THAT OPENED UP ETERNAL LIFE FOR ALL MANKIND

THE CROSS AND THE CRUCIFIXION

GRACE DOLA BALOGUN

About the Author

Grace Dola Balogun graduated from Fordham University Graduate School of Religion and Religious Education in the year 2010 with an M.A. in Religion and Religious Education. She has been a prayer mentor and advisor for many Christians of all denominations since 1988.

Visit her online at:
gracereligiousbookspublishers.com
Prayerstrengthforlife.com
Spiritpower.info
salvationcompleted.com
Facebook
GSTwitter@prayersource

To Order This Book

To order additional copies of this book,
please E-mail:
info@gracereligiousbookspublishers.com

This book may also be ordered from 30,000
wholesalers, retailers, and booksellers in the
U. S., and in Canada and over
100 countries globally.

To contact Grace Dola Balogun for an
interview or a speaking engagement,
please E-mail:
info@gracereligiousbookspublishers.com

The Spirit and the bride say, "Come!"
And let the one who hears say, "Come!"
Let the one who is thirsty come;
and let the one who wishes take
the free gift of the water of life.

Revelation 22:17

MARANATHA!

COME, LORD JESUS!

www.ingramcontent.com/pod-product-compliance
Lightning Source LLC
Chambersburg PA
CBHW021822090426
42811CB00032B/1975/J